Born in Amman, Jordan, Khaled Hazem Nusseibeh is a Jordanian-Palestinian whose family hails from Jerusalem. The Nusseibeh family is distinguished for being the custodian of the key of the Church of the Holy Sepulchre—a function it has held for a number of centuries. He is a graduate of Columbia and Princeton universities where he studied Political Science and Near Eastern Studies respectively. He has authored several books of poetry and prose and has been a translator for over 20 years.

To God Almighty and to His Messenger Muhammad, the
beacon of truth, enlightenment, and peace.

Khaled Hazem Nusseibeh

IN THE SWEET NIGHT

AUSTIN MACAULEY PUBLISHERS™
LONDON • CAMBRIDGE • NEW YORK • SHARJAH

ISBN – 9789948825470 – (Paperback)
ISBN – 9789948825463 – (E-Book)

Application Number: MC-10-01-4385974
Age Classification: E

Printer Name: iPrint Global Ltd
Printer Address: Witchford, England

First Published 2022
AUSTIN MACAULEY PUBLISHERS FZE
Sharjah Publishing City
P.O Box [519201]
Sharjah, UAE
www.austinmacauley.ae
+971 655 95 202

I wish to thank many people who have stood by me over the years, too many to mention by name. I am grateful to my parents, family, wife, teachers, sheikhs, colleagues, and associates.

I would like to thank my friend, Oussama Kanaan, for giving me moral and intellectual support over more than thirty years, being an avid connoisseur of literature and poetry and a man of culture.

Introduction

Addressing topical and timely significant issues represents a major defining characteristic of Khaled Nusseibeh's poetry in the last two decades or so. This is very well exemplified in his poem entitled "Corona" in the present collection. Nusseibeh admirably uses his poem to expose Nietzsche's well-known blasphemous declaration of the death of God in his *Zarathustra* book of 1884. The poet invites us in this poem to ponder upon the fate of human beings as they face Corona, which he describes as "insidious pestilence," without abiding by faith as the only conceivable tool of deliverance from the devastating consequences of the pandemic. Indeed, one couldn't agree more with Nusseibeh that it is only through holding on to faith, as the poem most eloquently reveals, that humanity can be saved from Corona, which has displayed how helpless human beings are without divine intervention.

Faith, as a matter of fact, figures as a recurring motif in several poems in the collection: "In the Sweet Night," "Seasonal Movement," "Prelude," "Irritation," and "Olive Branch." One gets the feeling that besides being used as a main topic, faith serves as a main source of inspiration which counterbalances the somber tone which marks the mode of representation in some poems, particularly "Corona" and "Golden Cage." In "Golden Cage," the poet revisits the pandemic using it this time to present his personal philosophical reflections on the human condition. Interestingly, "Golden Cage" is reminiscent of the pet shop in Ghada Al-Samman's *Beirut Nightmares*, insofar as it portrays the suffering of the birds in the cage in the age of Corona in the same way the pets take the toll of the Lebanese Civil War. The point is that in the novel and the poem human beings do not fare better than animals in front of great calamities – they are equally helpless. To highlight human life's vulnerability in the face of the "storm" of Corona, Nusseibeh resorts to using alliteration as an artistic stylistic device which enhances the reader's perception of humans' moral plight and weakness as they try to come with grips with the horrific disease: Truly life is like a fresh and fair flower. In its frailty, life here is likened to a "fresh and fair flower."

Just as Nusseibeh introduces faith as a bulwark of humans' defense against the fatal attack of Corona, he also presents strongly entrenched belief in everlasting life in the other world to mitigate human beings' concerns and worries about the transience of human life in this world. Nusseibeh devotes two of his poems "Revolving Door" and "The Ferris Wheel" to delve deeply into the juxtaposition of the transience of meaningless human life in this world with the glorious everlasting eternity in the other world. He uses the titles of the two poems as very effective extended metaphors to present his spiritual contemplation of the issue at length. In addition to his extensive use of imagery in these two poems to produce meaning effect, he remarkably employs balance to stress further the two poems' main themes. In "Revolving Door" we read: It is the manifest truth, irrationally denied, reasonably affirmed/ In the valleys of life, fellow travelers, we walk. In "The Ferris Wheel" Nusseibeh introduces the following balance: If only the human could well understand the transience of the present/ Pregnant with future's possibility, but alas overwhelmingly evanescent.

The two poems "A Question" and the "Will to Power" furnish more examples of Nusseibeh's characteristic interest in using balance as an effective stylistic device to the end of driving home a specific theme. In "A Question," through the use of balance, the reader becomes aware of the resourcefulness and versatility of human beings in using rudimentary tinsels for a wide range of purposes: To defend, to attack, to withdraw. In a context related to Israel's occupation of Palestine here is how balance is used to portray the

Israeli's attempt to break the Palestinians' deeply embedded will to power. By force Israel: dispossesses, arrogates, denies, confiscates, demolishes, and kills.

The use of pathetic fallacy in Nusseibeh's poetry adds to the wide scope of artistic stylistic devices he employs to express his sentiments and thoughts in the most forceful manner. For instance in the poem "Tillerman" we read: The boughs of trees of life moan /Inordinate suffering of people is verily endemic. In "Sacred Sanctuary" we come across a very touching example of pathetic fallacy which portrays the sorrowful image of the lonely holy Black Stone in Kaaba during Haj in the age of Corona: The holy Black Stone bemoans/ The woeful absence of the worshippers.

To conclude, I would like to draw attention to another defining feature of Nusseibeh's poetry, namely the modernist turn which gives his poetry one of its noticeable distinctive characteristics. This is well exemplified in the wide range of unconventional topics dealt with in his poetry. In a typical modernist fashion, Nusseibeh does not hesitate to use all sorts of unconventional topics as suitable subject matter for his poetry, including, for example, tennis, revolving door, irritation, teenage, wedding, etc. In doing so Nusseibeh, it would seem, is keen to adhere to the well-known modernist slogan: "Make It New," which is further emphasized in his peculiar interest in exploring new sources of imagery throughout the collection of poems.

Nedal Al-Mousa
Professor of English Literature

In the Sweet Night

I do not accept that I cannot hear her in the sweet night
Under the starry moonlit sky

Impossible to succumb to her ended journey in the
morning and eve
How she bequeathed a noble and astounding trail

I see her, awake and in a vision, walking a seemingly
long distance
In the direction of the fayha house of worship

Attired in a splendid light green gown
Smiling joyfully and exuding an overpowering
compassion

'Tis I that I have yet to traverse the distance to fayha
Dear beloved heaven for which I plaintively yearn

I am at the first step of a white marble staircase
Wearing heavy muddied boots

As if signifying the error and sinfulness of my
condition
That I must sincerely return to Him and repent

This, fellow human, is the imperative for all
To walk humbly in the valley of faith

A prelude to an isthmus preceding Judgment Day
When all shall be resurrected from the innumerable
graves

Dearest Fatima, I cannot admit that we have parted
Yet I passionately long for a day of union

In eschatological abode where a mere tiny moment
Is superior to the entirety of earthly life.

Seasonal Movement

O how miserable is the flu and the cold
Can I ask which of the seasons inaugurates life?

Veritably the rains of the cold season feed the hungry
earth
Without the process fruits are not made

Can I perhaps surmise about the favorite season?
The indomitable force of seasonal movement makes
irrelevant my pondering

As the years pass on, the bones beckon the warmth
Which the youthful need, albeit to a lesser degree

Splendid is every season of the Lord's Creation
'Tis better to thank, praise and worship

Fallen and vanquished are those that object
To His merciful purposes in life

The hour shall definitely arrive
When the wicked will stand in absolute meekness in
God's hell

If only, when they could in life, performed a prayer
Or accepted without denial the Message of God

Or spent a bushel of wheat to succor the indigent
Or refrained from blaspheming His Holy Name

The day has drawn nigh so anchor at mercy's port
A time so often in the past foretold

Relative to thee, O Lord, in your glory and majesty
I am as a water droplet under a horse's hoof

Or a resplendent warm ray of sun
That inexorably fades without trace

Or the dried drop of blood of a martyred soul
That relinquished all for your Greatness

I have toiled to successfully repent
Amid the unrelenting force of the earthly self

And have broken the repentance a thousand times
For contrition is lacking in sincerity

A negligence overpowers me thereby hindering
The soul in its glowing yearning of true love

I am, O Lord, the receding wave of water
Smashed by an indomitable tide

Undergirded by a formidable force of love
Animating the conduct of belligerent men

Forgive me, Lord, for the enormities
Sins that have marred the evanescent moment of life

I yearn for a warm garden of red roses
Their blood-like color turning into white

Allow me to water the embattled seed of faith
To wash away from my brow the dregs of soil

I seek love's masters to guide my staggering faith
To circle around a hearth of burning passion

Kindle the fire of affinity and love
And banish the drivers of sorrow and hate

Rancor has no place in a lush green field
Supporting grass, daffodils and countless flowers

If beauty has a moment of permanence
It is when the Eternal God is truly venerated

By hearts that have seen the Glorious Lord
And recognized His never-ending Truth

With shame, O Lord, I confess to Thee my sinfulness
Allow me to embrace your noble friends

Those that have spent tearful nights
With eyes dried of water

The elixir of living that Thou hath created
Without partners or earthly and celestial support

For You have inaugurated life in the beginning
And decree its veritable end

To be followed by the great Day of Judgment
When all life will be resurrected anew

On the vessel of transient life I sail
However the strength of the wind, expel me not from
Your Mercy.

Tennis

In broad daylight I witnessed
An epic match of tennis

Perhaps the time was around five decades ago
In a full stadium in the splendid Cairene Gezira Club

Situated in the verdant area of Zamalek
Straddled by the borders of the great river Nile

A prodigious Australian player fought ferociously
Perhaps he lost the match

The successful in life fight for every point
Ever alert to the possibility of defeat

In the incipient stages of the match it was possible to
rapidly run
To speed to reach a lob to save the point

Or to make amazing placement shots
Or to fight to break the serve

A mind wonders whether luck is the decisive factor
Or skill honed by relentless practice

In any event, tennis is a splendid sport
Which may arouse the passionate interest of young and
old alike.

Prelude

A rainy day may be variously perceived
A time of hardship or the prelude to abundance

We humans have harbored diverse attitudes
Those of hope and anticipation, and those of a grim
view

Achievement is oft the condition of the optimists
Exuding a positive energy that makes positive things
happen

Looking forward to a bright future
Even if the path is beset by obstacles

Which may be conceived of as challenges
To be made yielding by a stronger will

Whatever the clear and treacherous pathways of life
Despair must not dwell in the human heart

An organ that pulsates with the love of God
And feels joy and happiness with the great and modest

Truly, those that walk the path of faith
Shall reap vast rewards in eschatological time.

Communication of Love

Perforce to dive into the deeper regions
Of an immense and unfathomable unconscious

Perchance can one grip firm a distant reality?
If only the quest is more intense?

O how sweet is the ascent from the bed of the water
To then recover a deep and comfortable breath

Holding in hand an object that had sunk
Happily to a distance that is by some effort accessible

By digging deeper, a hollowness one might find
Or the substance of an immortal truth

To be known, not by a consciousness in abeyance
But by striving for a sublime reality

For the deeper the dive
The more dazzling the bezels of pearl to be found

Precious stones of wisdom, affirming, testifying
In unknowable communication of love and faith.

Tillermen

The sky of human society is overcast
With the scourge of war, exile, famine and pestilence

The little-knowing servant of God wonders:
Are we living in the times of the latter day?

The boughs of the trees of life moan
Inordinate suffering of people is verily endemic

Can the boughs drying from thirst be revived?
Given nourishment for vital resuscitation?

Sacred, fellow men, is human life
To be preserved and protected as a holy temple

The earth spawns all that is good
To be tended by the wise and free tillermen

Those that nurture life and sow the seeds of peace
And strive that none go hungry, that the sick are healed

Blessed are the tillermen that cast the fishing net
Catching and sharing all that is good

Defending life and nurturing freedom
In life's unfolding and evanescent moment

When the sky is overcast, the downpour is inescapable
But folks can help to make lodging safe.

Bidding Teenage Farewell

Is it not a joyous watershed
In the life of the lovely twins bidding teenage farewell?

For me and the mother, they are luminous stars
Adorning a great fairytale

Rife with both the challenging and the enjoyable
In a family's quest to live and progress

With great love and sacrifice, Suhaila exerted
monumental effort
To raise the beloved twins to be healthy and righteous

Shunning decadence and making good academic
progress
To be prepared for the long life ahead

On the trail of existence we tread
Counting the Lord's blessings and enduring life's trials

Zeinab and Sara for long brought joy to the family
And supplication is made for God to give them future
happiness

In the meandering trajectories of life's movement
The hope is for their steps to be firm
To–in effect –surmount the challenges that abound
To try to make wise choices with faith in Divine
Providence

Prayers are made for the longevity of wonderful Hazem
and Qadar
And Aunt Lina who gave to them so much love

And likewise long life for Lamia and Jaweed and Lama
Lights that shine in our horizon

On this day of December first we mark a milestone
In the life of a family in splendid Jordan

And affirm the great roots of Jerusalem and Nablus
And likewise those of great Syria.

The Will to Be

Time unfolds slowly and painfully
As the hunger strike heroes endure
Perseveringly defying the forces of imprisonment and
hunger
To raise above the highest horizons freedom's banner
The jail cell verily cannot alter the essential truth
Of unjust dispossession and occupation
The soldiers of Palestine, male and female, child and
elderly
Have greatly endured, that the dormant nation awakens
and lives
To rise from a stagnant condition of stupor
To meet the grave challenge of its great destiny
Beyond the message of aching empty intestines
Is an ominous signal to humanity in its entirety
The peace of the world hinges on the imperative of
resolution
Of the great tragedy of the Palestinian people
Thirst and hunger may not territorial restoration
achieve

But perchance may awaken a global conscience
And that of an occupying power which by force
Dispossesses, arrogates, denies, confiscates, demolishes
and kills

And yes incarcerates those that demand freedom
And restoration of legitimate rights
The will to be shall overcome
The forces of defeat and surrender.

Revolving Door

Perhaps entering the twilight zone is still a distance
away
Yet, the sense of finitude is powerfully thrust upon us
The mystifying revolving door of evanescent life
Welcoming the newcomers and inexorably bidding
others farewell
In the face of this reality of indomitable power
The heart and mind are driven to ponder myriad
questions
It is the manifest truth, irrationally denied, reasonably
affirmed
That the Great God created life for a purpose
Encapsulated in the notion that we were but created to
worship God
To engage in life's endless paths and pursuits, to
venerate and obey Him
And vitally important is the truth that the present finite
moment is a prelude
To a life of never-ending existence
For those that seek everlasting youth and joy

Seize the moment, plant the seed, seek His guidance
and mercy
In the valleys of life, fellow travelers, we walk
But we shall also inescapably walk in the valley of
death
Holding our heads up high by submission to Him
Ay, the Maker of all who treaded the earth, and who
will in future
Let us behold the rapidly moving revolving door
Making sure to access the exits of safety
Whatever the pain and anguish –and yes the happiness
of the journey

Let's yearn for an anchorage of safety and peace.

Recovery

Our close and distant horizons are beclouded
By events disturbing our calm

Those significant happenings to which one can only
succumb
Praying, supplicating, and yes, hoping for positive
eventualities

Anticipation of possible remedy
Cure that betters a trying circumstance

Of prolonged suffering visiting one with tremendous
will
Whom destiny has visited with extreme tribulation

As though challenging an invincible determination to
survive
Amid the unsettling winds of powerful force

The body is tested but the good cheer endures
As if inexorably conferring the comic on the painful

Suffering that buffets a physical being
But stands helpless in the face of a positive psychic
force

We patiently await imminent reunion
That marks the closure of a painful chapter.

The Ferris Wheel

At a solemn moment of reflection
Life's saga is comparable to an indomitable Ferris
Wheel
If only the human could well understand the transience
of the present
Pregnant with future's possibility, but alas
overwhelmingly evanescent
Have not all empires witnessed the vanishing moment
The inescapable tryst of bidding glory farewell?
Just like individuals, nations, and tribes
That entered life's gate only to make a final, ineluctable
exit
Fortune's wheel keeps company with men, while living
But people descend, surely and inevitably from the
wheel
Only to give way to the new wave of riders
Wise, or misled by the illusion of the passing,
eventually ending moment
If only life's true wisdom is discerned
That solely to God is eternal Glory

The Great Creator that originates and sustains life
Merciful, Almighty, without beginning or end
Happy and blessed are those that till the soil of eternal
life
Ushered in by God's Day of Resurrection
When humans will be from the graves brought forth
And when God will Judge all that lived
Who rode the illusory Ferris Wheel of earthly life.

Olive Branch

Perchance a person brandishing a sword
Is holding tightly to an olive branch

In the annals of human history so much grief was
avoidable
Prevented by the counsel of wise men and good
conscience

Singing merrily is the chorus of veritable joy
Celebrating en masse the coming of a fine hour

When fallen tears punctuate a feeling of truthfulness
Where deceit and falsehood are decisively overcome

Naught is more important than marking the moment of
faith
When primordial instinct is powerfully affirmed

By prostration and works of righteousness
Undergirding the brotherhood of humanity

Let's not sing a tune of morbid suffering
But instead chant an ode to joy.

A Rainy Day

A continuing weather depression besets the land
Bringing abundant rainfall and cold temperatures

While descending from a small, quaint building in
Rabieh
The asphalted uneven road lies in proximity

And an unpaved ground is drenched in mud
By virtue of the downpours of rain

A creature of the feline type is slouching
On the engine cover of a small Japanese car

Presumably because the engine was recently used
And provides warmth to the brown and white cat

The car is parked astride a yellow pavement
Across a building housing the Zeinab clan

For years splendid neighbors hailing from the city of
Salt
Who, across the years, multiplied in number to fill their
dwellings
The Amman day is dreary and the sky gray
But the journey to the workplace is a must.

Earthenware

A moment of immense value
When a family gathers around a meal

Cooking in earthenware punctuating the event
Pots of delectable and amazing food

A powerful tribute to all who nurture life
Strongly underpinning the life of civilization

A warm and comfortable den needn't be elusive
Knock man on the gates of earthly mercy

Heaven knows the innumerable errors
Mistakes that may be decidedly rectified

The sacred waters may join together
Erecting an edifice of sound living

Confront strongly the temptation of deviance
And walk on a straight path even if limping

Unthinkable and alien is infallibility
The moral is to rise after falling down.

Pearls

Like dazzling pearls of a cohesive necklace
A line of prophets across the ages

Preaching bezels of wisdom and truth
And conveying God's unitary dogma

Rise O mankind, O tribe, O nation
Harken to your Great Lord

The Creator of the totality of existence
Universes, nations, and worlds

Embrace the monotheistic idea of a unique God
And worship none but He

Multitudes were saved by accepting this Truth
While innumerable others walked the path of
damnation

The prophets were sent a mercy to mankind
To guide those who went astray

Some tribes and nations were smitten for disavowing
the truth
As a prelude to eternal torment and hellfire

Rise to the call O fellow brother, sister
For God has promised the believer everlasting solace
and joy

Great dwellings under which rivers flow
Eternal joy promised by the Lord of the worlds.

A Sad Tale

In a land near and far
Secluded by barriers of rancor and ill-will

A sad tale is perennially told
Of the fine and great martyr of the land

Whose body bled in the final gasps of life
Allahu Akbar were the last words of utterance

The coffin was carried by throngs of indignant
mourners
Marauding the streets of the city towards the final
resting place

The martyr's body emitted a sweet aroma
Confirming the truthfulness of the death

In a land of defiance 'tis not the first or final
martyrdom
As long as freedom is denied, rights withheld

Never will the folks to indignity succumb
And liberty is less than a mile away

Rejoice mother of the blessed martyr!
You have given all and shall be in God's time crowned

In a world marking the triumph of justice
And a hereafter of everlasting joy.

Perchance

Perchance standing still at a moment of solemnity
Partaking in the funeral of a demised human soul

Thinking illusively the event is a remote eventuality
Verily, the calamity cannot happen to me!

The sermon of death is inexorably about another soul
The illusion is the permanence of earthly life

The warm hearth will continually glow
And the den is steeped in permanence

Fatal illness is presently unthinkable
I cannot be the subject of an imminent eulogy aside a
grave

'Tis impossible to part with family and friends
Relations that seem to defy evanescence!

The shroud of death cannot replace the elegant attire
I cannot dwell solitarily in an isolated tomb

'Tis impossible to hear the plaintive cries during the
dirge
People I knew, bidding me a final farewell

Life, friend, is a moving shadow
A fleeting moment to be transiently lived.

*(Umar Ibn Al-Khattab said: "Strive for this world as
though you will live forever, and strive for the
Hereafter as though you will die on the morrow.")*

Vision with a Flag

An experience strongly etched in long memory
In the magnificent land of Anatolia

A man ascends a motorcycle
Accelerating with great speed

Riding in a wooden cylindrical form
Unleashing a powerful centrifugal force

The young man's face is draped in a flag
Yet the motorbike stunningly stays the course

Without falling to the ground below
Mesmerizing all beholding the show.

Steps

Many a time peculiar dreams are seen
Visions straddling the border of the surreal and real

Much is incomprehensible in the deeper regions of the
unconscious
Oozing out in unfathomable forms

Challenging steps are surprisingly easily climbed
Leading to a substantial bland building

An elevated floor as though an indistinct hotel
But how does one descend to the boat?

The building anomalously is itself the boat
Or blends with it in an implausible reality

Thus vanishes the necessity of descent
To a boat docking on the pier

The dream meshes perhaps with another
Traversing a crowded and bustling urban area

Banners of Hussein are rife and palpable
People beckoning for supplications

The speedboat sails in the wavy Strait
Only to reach a standstill in a dark place with an
aperture

One is overcome by a feeling of distress
Awakening, the dream defies comprehension.

Crossroads

In a cold, dark and rainy evening
We proceed towards a gift store on a declension

The aim is to visit a friend newly wed
Bringing closer together the Hammouris and Bani
Hassan

Lines in the sand of life that have coalesced
In a bond of love, matrimony, and blessed cohabitation

Hailing from the historic cities of Hebron and Mafrak
Deeply etched in a rich and illustrious history

The car traverses the areas of Amman
To finally reach a modern, quaint building in the
Sweifieh area

The building's exterior is interlaced with elegant wood
And has an entrance in a basement garage

A silvery lift ascends to the first floor
Where we are greeted by the jovial couple

Young, professional, and of optimistic view
Looking forward to a long and happy life

Exquisite fruits and biscuits are served
Along with tasty and sweet tea

The moderately sized living area looks to the south
Brightly lit with white leather couches and a rug
A gift of "Monopoly" is delivered
Albeit the recipient "Rahma" is unfortunately absent

A young girl from an earlier marriage
Splendid and affable as girls can be

The conversation spanned myriad subjects
Focusing considerably on common friends

Cheers to a delightful Jordanian–Palestinian couple
May happiness in the world and the Hereafter be your
fate.

Uneasy Quietude

Amid an air of uneasy quietude
An afternoon in Sweifieh slowly unfolds

Telephone calls are successively received
Not entailing fruitful business activity

A graying middle-aged man enters the office smiling
Soliciting donations for a charitable cause

And "Jewells" calls distressed from Madaba
Informing that she is riding a bus to Amman

Verily, labor is a fulfilling engagement
Geared to making ends meet

The atmosphere in the office is chilly
Coldness mitigated by hot ventilation

A small Jordanian flag sits atop a black table
Abutting a blue leather couch

Noises of car engines and horns are audible
Though issuing from a moderate distance

The office is today minimally active
In the hope for greater business flow

An electric paper shredder stands on the brown carpet
Turned off and not much in use

A pile of paper sits on the computer table
Documents that were previously translated

And noise of papers issuing from the printer is audible
From the office nearby

Two nails on the wall may be seen
Where a painting by Mr. Manko used to hang

Two neon lights are fastened to the ceiling
Producing for the room ample light

Atop the wall-to-wall carpeting are three reddish rugs
Crafted by the Banu Hamida clans

Every Drop and Ray

If you have left my vision
Your memory will never wither away

To this will testify innumerable souls
And every raindrop and ray

Beguile me not treacherous life
Love is always a tiring tale and mirthful play

Blooming as though the sun never sets
On the great horizons of every day

Relish the moment the merry heart says
And make gloom and sorrow go away

I can't understand the moving shadows of life
How life quickly unfolds and doesn't stay

Do we build for nothingness and unrelenting mirages
Shouldn't we strive for a better play?

Drama that produces and concurrently reflects reality
To its indomitable power we cannot say "nay."

Bitter Companion

O sweet, bitter companion of us all
Who dwell in this earthly abode

Come near, draw far, come hither go thither
All have a tryst with the terrifying visitor

Abhorrent even though you are
You are but a veil that hides continuing life

An isthmus that midwifes eternal living
A tomb of great joy, or of tormenting darkness

I fear you not bitter, unconquerable enemy
Who vanquished the mightiest of generals, the greatest
of kings

Lurk you behind the curtain of every act
Awaiting equally the strong survivors and the feeble
creatures

Verily there's a Being that vanquishes finitude
The uncreated Living God

One without partner in the Heaven
Sovereign and Sustainer of all creation
O abhorrent night perhaps I do not fear you
For I trust in the Lord of Light.

Welcome Spring

Speechless and not knowing what to say
We had to bid spring farewell

But the indomitable force of youth moves on
Forcibly displacing defunct and atrophied living

Settled urban dwellers are forcibly uprooted
Catapulted into life in cold and makeshift tents

The children face a terrible challenge
War waged by the living night

Hunger abounds as does the quest for freedom
And for the essentials of decent and secure life

Constantly interrupted by the hurling of fire
Randomly ravaging the school, the clinic, the makeshift
tent

Lost for words, we cannot answer you beloved child

And noble mother condescendingly eyeing the mighty

A living hell has been foolishly produced
Engendering suffering of monumental proportions

Let the sirens scream for silence and quiet
To still the pernicious waves of the day

Let's hope together for a better morrow
When the mighty could, unperturbed, look into the
child's eyes.

Corona

An imperceptible Corona envelopes the great sun
Visible upon the onset of an amazing eclipse

And a frightening scourge is enveloping our great earth
As though brazenly challenging the "guardians" of life

Fellow men the freezing ice shall gradually melt
And the kind earth will once again gently embrace

Humans whose footsteps have been ominously heavy
Bringing peril to overwhelmed life

Stretching from the farthest east to the distant west
A scare has spread, perhaps more illusory than real

Many a time in the near and distant path
Humanity faced the specter of mortal threat

And the will to overcome ineluctably prevailed
Producing solutions to seemingly intractable challenge

But the stance must be that we cannot stand still
Observing our planet decidedly endangered

And the essential step is to revoke Nietzsche's dictum
Declaring for modernity the odious phrase that "God is
dead"

For God Almighty is Living and Pre-eternal
The true Omnipotent power of the great universe

And to produce peace and a salvaged civilization on
earth
We must make our peace with Him.

A Snake and a Chicken

Though transpiring decades ago
A scene indelibly imprinted on the memory

Forming an enduring but disturbing impression
In the mind of a child and adult

The venue is a sizeable impressive zoo
Containing innumerable wondrous creatures

In a small room one could see a huge snake
Beyond a thick and transparent glass

Upon the snake sits a pitiable chicken
Unaware that it is the snake's imminent meal

Having eyed this riveting scene
I moved to yet other rooms for additional viewing.

An Unruly Horse

On a bitter day in the distant past
When memories stand far away
On grassland I rode a restless horse
No sooner than I was nestled on the stirrup
The horse galloped erratically and without control
Bumping upon it up and down
I was catapulted to the ground
The body much ached and felt sore
But happily there were no broken bones
The incident was a snapshot from a powerfully held
memory
On a bitter day in the life of a growing child.

A Question

At times an unfathomable question arises
To answer it a restless soul must probe

And see the truth by un-turning heavy stones
That are in their places since time immemorial

Out of which tools were made
And rudimentary utensils and arms

To defend, to attack, to withdraw
With fear and awe inhabiting the heart

Plowshares were likewise made
To till the soil and prepare it for planting

Requiring toil, irrigation, and a will to produce
Yes, we shall reap the fruits whose seeds we sowed.

Sisters and Brother

Verily, affection for the sisters cannot be withheld
Companions on a lengthy track of life
Affable, noble, and of kind spirit
Etched in consciousness since early life
The lily that carried me whilst falling on a staircase
Enduring immense pain to protect a heedless child
And Lina the fine woman named after palm trees
Welcoming the broken poet with radiant red cherries
By God much of the path of life has been traversed
Watershed leading to another, to yet another
In dispersal the family is tightly net
Although evincing a somewhat tired look
Gone are the days of illusory youth
Having yielded to the indomitable force of time
And salutation to a beloved brother
A lifelong and jovial companion in a prolonged life
Scarred we all are in a tempestuous life
Undergirded by sometimes considerable turbulence
Happy may be the days of all in this family
Fathered and mothered by the great Hazem and Qadar

Fate brought us together and till death do us part
We shall keep the bonds of affinity and love.

Golden Cage

Even the mighty creatures have weakness
And the same applies to two splendid and colorful birds
Perched on a decrepit bamboo seat
Is a presently empty golden cage
Earlier standing in horizontal direction
Where the birds lived and sang
Wonder visits the mind whether the birds set free
Are still flying about or dead
The pondering is in a balcony crammed with assorted
objects
Chairs, a table, and plants of assorted kinds
A sweet mild wind gently blows
Bringing relief to tedium amid a strict curfew
Amman like the world is within the storm
Of the insidious pestilence of the COVID virus
Truly life is like a fresh and fair flower
To be beheld by a keen and perceptive eye
Courage Rome –the deep dark cloud shall pass
Lamentably leaving behind a terrible trail of death and
distress

In essence health is an illusory walking shadow
That has an inevitable tryst with ailment
The disease is to think life to be everlasting
When finitude is humanity's universal condition

Alas, for God's garden this man of sin yearns
In an abode of eternal joy

Manifesting the Lord's mercy in this trying world
And in the unending life of the Kingdom of God.

Soil

Could it be construed as such
The final sunrays on a tired soul?

The chap in a dream is descending the stairs
Of the rather old Saladin Mosque

Abutting a usually vivacious park
Rife with the bustling noise produced by playing
children

And mothers with toddlers in strollers
Perhaps conversing with other women

One side of the perimeter has much soil
As though signifying the possibilities of fecundity and
regeneration

The soil is where vehicles are ordinarily parked
Of inhabitants of the area and worshippers of the
mosque.

Two Paths

Seated in an aircraft packed with passengers
'Tis verily a befuddling situation

Is it a path of pain and sorrow
Apparently a tortuous Via Dolorosa?

An hour of adversity is it
Or a sufferable trial after which ease ensues?

An Indian dignitary walks in the aisle
Aiming for a destination at the rear of the plane

Dear life, so innumerable are your trajectories
Endless possibilities of unfolding and previous life

The gentleman reaches the aircraft stair
Near the end of which is a plethora of gold

Rows of rings methinks signifying union
Or perhaps abundance of untold proportion.

Irritation

Every human is irked in his unfolding life
Irritated by perhaps not so significant a matter

And indeed at times the trial is great
Testing the fortitude and endurance of a soul

The purpose is for one not to think
That God's heaven could be on earth

The quests for utopias and dystopias have been
Usually experiences of immeasurable suffering

Witness Pol Pot's zero hour
Leaving behind a horrific trail of genocide and
destruction

Or Lenin's regime of the leadership of the proletariat
Erecting a system contrary to the instincts and nature of
history

That said, one yearns for an improved condition
A world of faith, peace, and justice

Imagine all the people living in substantial harmony
Shunning corruption and hedonism, building structures
of solace.

Watershed

Existential anguish brings upon powerful yearning
The search for a vortex of truth

What is life's essential meaning?
And wither the unfathomable trajectories of the future?

Is there truly eschatological reality?
A life after corporeal death and material decomposition

If life has teleological purpose
Then how must I behave in earthly life?

How can suffering on earth be explained?
Pestilence, illness, poverty, and wars

If humans have a spiritual aspect
Can we define and fathom spirit?

Does a good, just, and merciful God exist?
The Omnipotent Creator of the world

If the landing at a safe port is desired
Then Islam, fellow men, is the way

If people yearn for safe journeying and passage
Then let Muhammad, brother of Moses and Jesus, be
your guide

Earthly life is a flickering light that rapidly twilights
So let's make haste in obeying the Lord's commands

Enshrined in the Holy Quran and the Prophet's Sunnah
And the exemplary model of the early generations

Indubitably, amid deep darkness the light of God shall
shine
Illuminating the ways of East and West.

Sacred Sanctuary

The holy Black Stone bemoans
The woeful absence of the worshippers

You see, the insidious virus has impeded
The penitent flock from circumambulation

The repentant noble Englishman, the aboriginal lady
That have found the Lord and their true essence

The Kaaba, though speechless and without hearing
Awaits the faithful multitudes on Abraham's path

At its environs we shed our impure attire
Innumerable sins committed in the ephemeral world

O Lord I answer your sacred command
And bear witness that there is no partner to thee

The sole Creator of vast existence
The Maker of earthly and eschatological life

Woe to those who follow the Prophets' nemesis
The accursed Beelzebub that deceives to lead people
astray

He verily is shorn of power over the faithful
The testifiers of the principal cosmic truth

I witness to the unicity of God
None but He we worship

In its solitude the blessed Kaaba is tearful
Sad that the flock are a distance afar.

Sanitarium

Remembrances entail the cheerful and painful
Falling over and bruising a fragile knee

Walking down an asphalted slope
One's strength yielded to a tormenting accident

With difficulty one in adolescent years was transported
To a sanitarium in an old and distinguished school

What if it was one of hundreds of falls?
One's suffering fades amid the others' inordinate woes

The homeless, the destitute, those with terminal illness
Those without marital companion or supporting
offspring

The woes of life are verily relative
The sound of mind count the blessings with gratitude to
the Almighty God

The shining literati of the English pithily said
All's well that ends well

The essence of the matter is to believe whilst suffering
And to grow the wiser in the process

Like life pain is inexorably transient
On the plains of an evanescent life

Whatever harm may be in store for the living
Those of inveterate cynicism are the lifeless
Dead of a conscience in need of revival
To perceive that life has definite purpose.

Stairway to Heaven

There is a way to unmatched solace
The delights of proximity to God

Am I a tiny drop of water
Or a speck of dust in the vast universe?

Waveringly treading the greatest path
The road of glorification of the Lord

Muhammad and Christ charted the course
Affirming the unfathomable seas of Divine love

We are an insignificant being in vast oceans
Whirling in a dance of worldly aim

The true essence underpins the quest
A sincere intention of spiritual devotion

The heart sinks at the mention of the Holy Name
Allah, One, Beautiful, Omnipotent and Merciful

Help me dear Lord in my quest to know Thee
Beholding omnisciently all that exists

And without partner sustaining existence
In all its facets of matter and spirit

Permit me humbly to express surrender to Thee
Having discovered imperfectly that you are the sole
Creator
One in Essence, Names, and Attributes
Glorious, Pre-eternal and Loving.

Beloved Lebanon

'Tis like a gem that is ephemerally damaged
With hemorrhaging amid wanton destruction

Scenes of terrible carnage punctuate a horrid scene
Of desolation visited on an ancient land

The sky of beloved Lebanon is overcast with heavy
clouds
Bringing moroseness to the far-flung world

But those in the know recognize the small country's
thistles
Which if trodden upon makes the aggressor pay a dear
price

Abode of Christianity, Islam, and ancient Phoenicia
Which helped significantly write the annals of a great
history

The terrible explosion brought down tall and short
structures
Producing a mesmerizing scene of apocalyptic
proportions

Future suffering may be definitively averted
When in unison the forces of dissension are overcome

And when a great people compose a covenant for
genuine unity
And chart a future of great hope

The cedar tree shall forever adorn Lebanon's horizon
However much the thorns bloody the splendid shoreline

Lebanon sends to the world a message of peace
Amid the great torment of its unfolding tragedy.